The
Joy
Journal

The
Joy
Journal

with the Geranium Lady—Barbara Johnson

WORD PUBLISHING
Dallas·London·Vancouver·Melbourne

J. Countryman is a registered trademark
of Word Publishing, Inc.

A J. Countryman Book

Designed by Dennis Hill

Compiled and edited by Terri Gibbs

ISBN 0-8499-5272-7

Printed and bound in the United States of America

6 7 8 8 RRD 9 8 7 6 5 4 3 2 1

Introduction

I created this zippy, zany journal as a fun way to record the moments of sunshine and happiness in life. But why record them in a book? Because you are what you think. Philippians 4:8 tells us, "Think about the things that are true and honorable and right and pure and beautiful and respected." If you think on joy and laughter, your heart will be filled with a sunny smile. How do you inspire thoughts of joy? You fill your surroundings with joy.

This *Journal* is a new way for you to add joy to your life. When good things happen to lighten your load and brighten your day, write them down. When someone pays you a compliment, write it down. When you remember nice things from the past, write them down. Let the journal become a personal treasure chest—your collected thoughts of hope, gladness, and love.

When you start to collect joy, you will find it's like a magnet. Joy is everywhere. All you have to do is look for it and use it instead of saving it for Sunday-Best. And that is precisely what this journal will help you do, because recording joyful thoughts has a way of making you look for joyful things.

If you find yourself slipping into the clutches of drudgery, pessimism, and gloom, this *Joy Journal* can help you stay in a frame of mind that celebrates life instead of letting it simply go by or becoming bogged down in the miseries. It will help you develop a sense of humor. It will bring a smile to your face and hope to your heart. This will be a treasury of gladness to inspire you for years to come.

Barbara Johnson

A smile is the light in the window of your face that shows that your heart is at home.

Doing something kind for someone is a great way to feel good about yourself.

Make a list of things you could do for specific people that would bring them "splashes of joy."

1. _____

2. _____

3. _____

4. _____

5. _____

6. _____

7. _____

8. _____

Happiness is elusive and can be wiped out in a second, but abiding joy from the Lord is like a deep river down in your heart that just keeps flowing.

An attitude of gratitude rids our lives of the film of frustration, the rust of resentment, and the varnish of vanity—all destroyers of self-esteem.

_____

_____

_____

_____

_____

_____

_____

When we count our blessings, we multiply harmony and good feelings.

_____

_____

_____

_____

_____

When we allow God to work within us . . .
we become sparkling jewels that beautify His
kingdom.

Joy Notes—Write the words to a song that always brings you joy.

_____

_____

_____

_____

_____

_____

_____

_____

_____

_____

_____

_____

_____

_____

_____

_____

I believe laughter is like a needle and thread. Deftly used, it can patch up just about everything.

One day I shall burst my buds of calm and blossom into hysteria.

Have character. Don't be one.

_____

_____

_____

_____

_____

_____

_____

_____

_____

Smile! It kills time between disasters.

_____

_____

_____

_____

_____

Remember: "Where there is no control, there is no responsibility." Here are some ridiculous excuses to justify carrying those burdens of guilt. Can you think of one or two to add?

1. If I don't carry this load of guilt, I won't have an excuse for that extra ten pounds on the bathroom scale.
2. Someone's got to be guilty. It might as well be me.
3. If I laid down all this guilt somewhere I might forget where I put it.

4. _____

_____

5. _____

_____

6. _____

_____

Worry is wasting today's time to clutter up tomorrow's opportunities with yesterday's troubles.

_____

_____

_____

_____

_____

_____

_____

Faith makes the uplook good, the outlook bright, the inlook favorable, and the future glorious.

_____

_____

_____

_____

_____

_____

If you carry the burdens of others, you lose your own.

Love makes the world go 'round, but laughter keeps you from getting dizzy.

Memo:

Don't worry, I won't forget you. I've written your name on the palm of my hand.

God

(Isaiah 49)

Laugh and the world laughs with you. Cry and you simply get wet!

_____

_____

_____

_____

_____

_____

_____

_____

_____

_____

_____

_____

_____

_____

_____

_____

_____

There are three ways to get something done:

1. Do it yourself.

2. Hire someone to do it.

3. Forbid your kids to do it.

Laughter is like a shock absorber that eases the blows of life.

_____

_____

_____

_____

_____

_____

_____

_____

_____

_____

_____

_____

_____

_____

_____

_____

_____

Humor is God's weapon against worry, anxiety, and fear.

Since it takes forty-three muscles to frown but only seventeen muscles to smile, why not conserve energy?

_____

_____

_____

_____

_____

_____

_____

An optimist laughs to forget;
the pessimist forgets to laugh.

_____

_____

_____

_____

_____

Joy Notes—Write down some of your favorite joy verses from the Bible.

_____

_____

_____

_____

_____

_____

_____

_____

_____

_____

_____

_____

_____

_____

_____

_____

_____

_____

Frogs have it easy: they can eat what bugs them.

_____

_____

_____

_____

_____

_____

_____

_____

_____

_____

_____

_____

_____

_____

I really believe laughter is the sweetest music that ever greeted the human ear.

Patience is the ability to count down before blasting off.

_____

_____

_____

_____

_____

_____

_____

_____

_____

_____

_____

_____

_____

_____

A sense of humor can help you overlook the unattractive, tolerate the unpleasant, cope with the unexpected, and smile through the unbearable.

Joy Notes—Record a special memory from your childhood that splashes you with joy!

_____

_____

_____

_____

_____

_____

_____

_____

_____

_____

_____

_____

_____

_____

_____

When you look at all the pain and problems in the world, creeping pantyhose isn't exactly a 7.2 on the Richter scale of human suffering.

It's a great comfort to know that
God has His hands on the
steering wheel of the universe.

To know and feel God's love is to know the deep kind of abiding joy that you want to splash all over others.

Laughter is like premium gasoline: it helps take the knock out of living!

_____

_____

_____

_____

_____

_____

_____

_____

Anything that makes us laugh in the face of life's adversity is valuable.

_____

_____

_____

_____

_____

_____

Memo:

You hang on to Jesus real tight, and you won't stay at the bottom; you'll get over the top!

Barbara

Tears begin your healing process, and laughter propels it along.

Laughter is nutrition for your soul, a tourniquet to stop the bleeding of a broken heart.

This life is short. It's the next one that lasts forever!

A sense of humor is connected to the way you look at life . . . the way you put your problems in perspective.

_____

_____

_____

_____

_____

_____

_____

_____

When you hit life's potholes—laugh.

_____

_____

_____

_____

_____

_____

When frustrations develop into problems that stress you out, . . . do something nice for yourself—not out of selfishness, but out of wisdom.

Make a list of some ways you will pamper yourself the next time you need a stress-buster.

1. Take a bubble bath. (An absolute must!)

2. _____

3. _____

4. _____

5. _____

6. _____

7. _____

8. _____

A lot of kneeling keeps one in good standing.

Humility is like underwear—
essential, but indecent if it shows.

Laughter may not get you out of your tunnel, but it will definitely light your way.

_____

_____

_____

_____

_____

_____

_____

_____

_____

_____

_____

_____

_____

_____

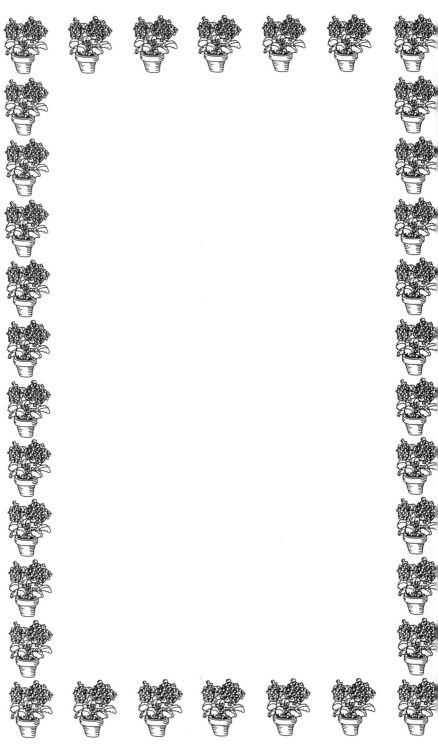

Sometimes it's hard to soar with the pigeons because of all the turkeys in your life.

_____
_____
_____
_____
_____
_____
_____
_____
_____

Winners turn stress into something good; losers let stress turn life into something bad.

_____
_____
_____
_____
_____

The only thing you can really control in this roller coaster called life is your own mental attitude.

God will never let you sink under your circumstances. He ALWAYS provides a safety net.

The only way to live happily with folks is to overlook their faults and admire their virtues.

Laughing together over life's little twists and turns is a great way to let off steam and keep stress at a minimum.

_____

_____

_____

_____

_____

_____

_____

_____

I don't have all the answers to life but I know Someone who does.

_____

_____

_____

_____

_____

The human spirit can survive pain, loss, death, taxes, and even wet pantyhose . . . and life goes on.

Joy Notes— Write about a time when someone made a special effort to splash joy all over your life. Remember how good you felt and use that memory to brighten your day.

_____

_____

_____

_____

_____

_____

_____

_____

_____

_____

_____

_____

_____

_____

_____

_____

_____

I know a little suffering is good for the soul, but somebody must be trying to make a saint out of me!

When a woman is gloomy,

everything seems to go

wrong; when she is cheerful,

everything seems right!

Proverbs 15:15 TLB

The same sun hardens mud and softens wax.
Trials can either break us or make us.

Every flower that ever bloomed had to go
through a whole lot of dirt to get there!

If a lion's roar isn't getting you anyplace, try a bear hug.

Memo:

Remind me to tell you about the plans I have for your life.——By the way, they're plans to give you a future and a hope.

God

(Jeremiah 29)

Never let a problem to be solved become
more important than a person to be loved.

Floods of adversity may sweep over us, but only so that the light of His presence may shine upon us.

_____

_____

_____

_____

_____

_____

_____

_____

_____

Shared joy is a double joy. Shared sorrow is half a sorrow.

_____

_____

_____

_____

_____

Laughter is like jogging on the inside . . . or internal jogging I call it.

God often allows our hearts to be broken so He can beautify our lives.

A new month is always special to me. I like to celebrate wildly on the first day of the month by changing the bedsheets, taking a leisurely bubble bath, and doing FUN things just for myself. It's a celebration, a way of LOOKING for the joy and CHOOSING to be happy.

Write down some fun things that would help you celebrate and LOOK FOR THE JOY.

1. _____

2. _____

3. _____

4. _____

5. _____

6. _____

7. _____

8. _____

If there were no grief to hollow our hearts,
there would be no room for joy!

It's not so much what happens to you; it's how you handle the happenings.

The best exercise for good relationships is bending over backward.

You cannot control the past, but you can ruin a perfectly good present by worrying about the future.

_____

_____

_____

_____

_____

_____

_____

_____

_____

_____

_____

_____

_____

_____

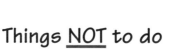

Things <u>NOT</u> to do
when you're feeling blue:

Don't weigh yourself.

Don't watch "Old Yeller."

Don't go near a
chocolate shop.

Don't open your credit
card bill.

Don't go shopping for
a new bathing suit.

When you get to the end of your rope, hang on to the hope.

_____

_____

_____

_____

_____

_____

_____

_____

The best gifts are tied with heartstrings—yours.

_____

_____

_____

_____

_____

_____

You never need an excuse to celebrate. Don't let one day go by without finding something to celebrate—even something others might think is insignificant.

Here are some of my suggestions. Why not add a few of your own?

1. The flowers are finally blooming in your backyard.

2. You finish the sweater you've been knitting for the last six months.

3. You balance your checkbook.

4. You finish the laundry and all the socks come out in even pairs.

5. _____

6. _____

7. _____

8. _____

It's better to forget and smile than to
remember and be upset.

_____

_____

_____

_____

_____

_____

_____

_____

_____

_____

_____

_____

_____

_____

_____

_____

Memo:

Relax! You are not responsible for everything in the universe. That's still My job.

God

It never hurts your eyesight to look on the bright side of things.

_____

_____

_____

_____

_____

_____

_____

_____

Try a quick hug to cool a slow burn.

_____

_____

_____

_____

_____

The sound of laughter is God's hand upon a troubled world.

_____

_____

_____

_____

_____

_____

_____

_____

_____

_____

_____

_____

Take every opportunity to make
good memories—for yourself and
for others.

Faith is seeing light with your heart when all your eyes see is darkness.

Think about some wonderful things that could happen this year and smile:

1. Your husband remembers your birthday AND your anniversary, all in one year!
2. Your kids (or grandkids) go to bed the first time they are asked.
3. Your mother-in-law comes for dinner and your husband doesn't remind you what a great cook she is.
4. Your twenty-seven-year-old son comes down for breakfast and says, "Mom, I've got a job and I'm moving out on Friday."
5. Your teenager returns your car, washed, vacuumed, and full of gas!
6. Your doctor takes your blood pressure and his eyes don't get as big as saucers.
7. Your husband turns off the TV, serves you a cup of coffee and says, "What would you like to talk about?"

Now add a few serendipities of your own.

8. _____

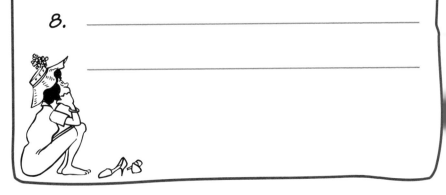

_____

9. _____

_____

10. _____

_____

11. _____

_____

12. _____

_____

13. _____

_____

14. _____

_____

15. _____

_____

Friends give each other gifts without ribbons
every time they get together, simply by
exchanging kindness and love.

Smile! It may not make you feel better, but it's sure to make someone else feel better.

I count my friends as timeless treasures that grow more beautiful each day.

_____

_____

_____

_____

_____

_____

_____

_____

_____

_____

My cooking advice to newlyweds is don't season your food with Old Spice.

_____

_____

_____

_____

_____

If you don't love, you'll find an excuse. If you do love, you'll find a way.

The twin sister of thankfulness is praise.

_____
_____
_____
_____
_____
_____
_____
_____
_____
_____
_____
_____
_____
_____
_____
_____

Laughter is like

changing a baby's diaper:

It doesn't permanently

solve any problems,

but it does make things

more acceptable for a while.

If you look hard enough, you can see the positive and even humorous side of anything.

With a positive attitude, tears of sorrow will
start to glisten with gladness.

_____

_____

_____

_____

_____

_____

_____

_____

Laughter is the sun that drives winter
from the human face.

_____

_____

_____

_____

_____

_____

Here are some JOY resolutions I set as goals for myself each year:

1. Avoid grumbling, particularly out loud.
2. Laugh out loud . . . and often.
3. Always greet folks with a smile.
4. Be an encourager.
5. Be thankful—especially for your family.

(What would you add to the list?)

6. _____

7. _____

8. _____

9. _____

10. _____

11. _____

12. _____

You can be as happy as you decide to be.

_____

_____

_____

_____

_____

_____

_____

_____

_____

_____

_____

_____

_____

_____

_____

_____

_____

Life is like an ice cream cone:
Just when you think you've got it
licked, it drips all over you!

God loves us too much to leave us stuck to the ceiling.

_____

_____

_____

_____

_____

_____

_____

_____

_____

_____

_____

_____

_____

_____

_____

_____

We can choose to gather

to our hearts the thorns

of disappointment, failure,

loneliness, and dismay

due to our present situation,

or we can gather the flowers

of God's grace, unbounding love,

and unmatched joy.

Friendship doubles our joys and divides our sorrows.

Hope comes out of knowing to whom you belong and knowing that He is in control.

Only some of us learn by other people's mistakes; the rest of us have to be the other people.

_____

_____

_____

_____

_____

_____

The soul would have no rainbows if the eyes had no tears.

_____

_____

_____

_____

_____

_____

_____

When I think of smells that made my childhood special, I remember running home for lunch rather than eating in the school cafeteria because we lived only three blocks away. The winter days in Michigan were cold and blustery, and I can still feel the crunch of the snow under my galoshes as I hurried home.

I'd run up the steps into our house, and as I came through the door, I'd smell that wonderful homemade tomato soup, made with my mother's special chili sauce, canned the summer before. The sauce was her own special blend, and along with onion, peppers, and tomatoes, of course, it made her soup unforgettable. How I'd love to come in out of the biting cold wind into that warm house and stand over the floor register, feeling that heat flow up around me. Then I'd sit down to a bowl of that steaming hot tomato soup. What a delight!

Write about a delicious smell or favorite dish that made your childhood special.

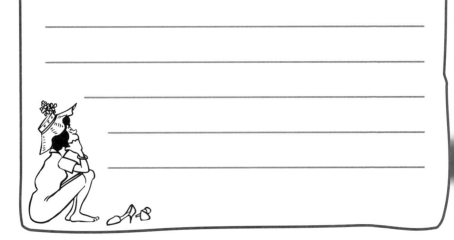

A good cry is a wet-wash, but a hearty laugh gives you a dry cleaning.

Look for the light of God that is hitting your life, and you will find sparkles you didn't know were there.

_____

_____

_____

_____

_____

_____

_____

_____

Humor is the shock absorber of life.

_____

_____

_____

_____

_____

_____

Memo:

About tomorrow—let God worry!

Barbara

A friend is one who strengthens you with prayers, blesses you with love, and encourages you with hope.

When stress closes in, your best move is to turn to the Lord.

Use what you have to enrich the lives of others, and you will soon find your own cup running over with joy.

Things aren't as bad as they seem . . .
sometimes they're even worse!

_____

_____

_____

_____

_____

_____

_____

_____

_____

_____

_____

_____

_____

_____

Flowers can even grow on dung
hills!

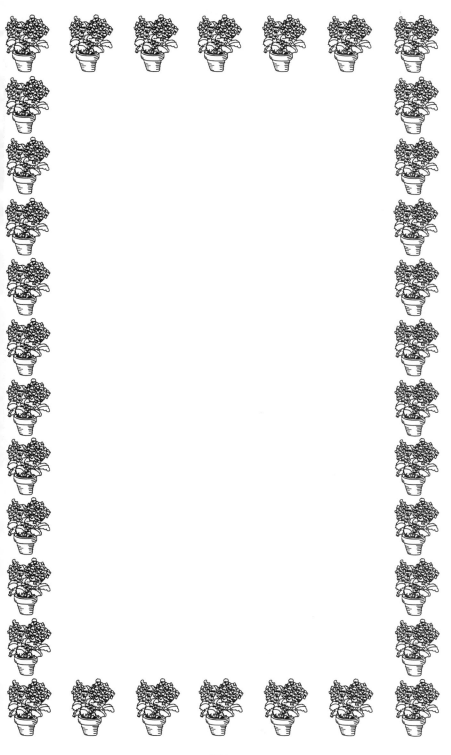

Joy Notes—Write how God has wonderfully answered some of your prayers. Read the list every now and then as a reminder of His faithfulness.

1. _____

2. _____

3. _____

4. _____

5. _____

6. _____

7. _____

8. _____

9. _____

10. _____

When we seek God with all our hearts, the gloomees don't have a chance!

An obstacle is like the hurdle

in a steeplechase:

rise up to it,

throw your heart over it,

and the horse

will go along too!

The surest mark of a Christian is not faith or love, but JOY.

_____

_____

_____

_____

_____

_____

_____

_____

People with time for others are happy all around the clock.

_____

_____

_____

_____

A little oil of Christian love will save a lot of friction.

_____

_____

_____

_____

_____

_____

_____

_____

_____

_____

_____

_____

_____

It doesn't take a dictionary to learn the language of love.

At day's end, I turn all my problems over to God—He's going to be up anyway.

_____

_____

_____

_____

_____

_____

_____

_____

_____

_____

_____

_____

_____

_____

If your faith cannot move mountains it ought to at least be able to climb them.

We need all the *amusing* grace we can get
from *God's* amazing, inexhaustible supply.

Faith never knows where it is being led, but it loves the One who is leading.

In God's economy, nothing is wasted—not one flicker of hope, not a single act of kindness, not one imponderable "Why?"

_____

_____

_____

_____

_____

_____

_____

_____

_____

_____

_____

_____

_____

_____

_____

Joy Notes—Learn to laugh even in the hard times. Think of three circumstances in your difficult situation that you can poke fun at—and laugh!

1. _____

   _____

2. _____

   _____

3. _____

   _____

   _____

The great beautifier is a contented heart and a happy outlook.

Adversity is the diamond dust Heaven uses to polish its jewels.

For every single thing that goes wrong in our lives, we have fifty to one hundred blessings.

_____

_____

_____

_____

_____

_____

_____

_____

Anxiety does not empty tomorrow of its sorrows, but only empties today of its strength.

_____

_____

_____

_____

_____

To love and be loved is to feel the sun from both sides.

If you want JOY for half an hour,
take a bubble bath.

If you want JOY for an afternoon,
go shopping.

If you want JOY for an evening,
go out to dinner.

If you want JOY for a day,
go on a picnic.

If you want JOY for a week,
go on a vacation
(or send the kids to camp).

If you want JOY for a month,
spend within your budget.

If you want JOY for life,
invest time in others.

Instead of wearing the galoshes of gloom, we need to wrap ourselves in the "garment of praise" (see Isaiah 61:3).

_____

_____

_____

_____

_____

_____

_____

_____

_____

_____

_____

_____

_____

_____

_____

_____

_____

If we say a situation is hopeless, we
are slamming the door in God's face.

God has only called you to be faithful.
He did not call you to be successful.

Blessed are the flexible for they shall not be bent out of shape.

Love is a magic doorway through which any soul may pass from selfishness to service.

Invent some silliness to put laughter in your life. Here are some of my suggestions, and you can add your own.

Have chocolate pie for breakfast.

Do <u>not</u> come in out of the rain.

Pop popcorn without putting the lid on.

Rip those tags off your new pillows!

_____

_____

_____

_____

_____

_____

_____

_____

_____

_____

_____

Prayer is asking for rain. Faith is carrying an umbrella.

If you are interested in the hereafter, remember that the HERE determines the AFTER!

There is no better exercise for the heart than reaching down and lifting someone up.

God is offering Himself to you daily, and the rate of exchange is fixed. It is your sins for His forgiveness, your tragedy and hurt for His balm of healing, and your sorrow for His joy.

Memo:

Trust me, I have everything under control.

Jesus

Regret has a way of trapping you in a rut that can become a deep hole of despair.

Life isn't always what you want, but it's what you've got; so, with God's help, CHOOSE TO BE HAPPY . . . !

The foundation of all joy for Christians is that we can live as though Christ died yesterday, rose today, and is coming tomorrow.

_____

_____

_____

_____

_____

_____

_____

_____

_____

_____

_____

_____

_____

_____

_____

If you want to make a friend, let someone do you a favor.

Thanks for
helping me
over the hump!

Some people continually change jobs, mates, and friends, but they never think of changing themselves.

_____

_____

No matter how gloomy life may seem, we can still count our blessings. Make a list of some of the wonderful things you have to be thankful for:

1. _____

2. _____

3. _____

4. _____

5. _____

6. _____

7. _____

8. _____

"I'm not ignoring the facts—I'm just looking at them and trying to find joy, not misery."

Yesterday is a canceled check, and tomorrow is a promissory note. But today is cash, ready for us to spend in living.

God will accept a broken heart, but He must have all the pieces.

God can take your trouble and change it into treasure.

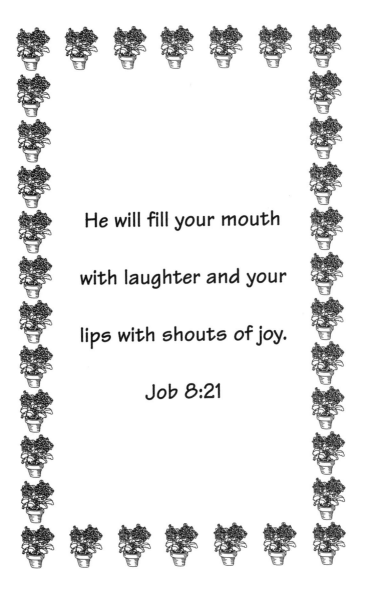

He will fill your mouth

with laughter and your

lips with shouts of joy.

Job 8:21

Hope for the best, be prepared for the worst,
and take what comes with a smile.

A genuine sense of humor is the pole that adds balance to our steps as we walk the tightrope of life.

When I look back at childhood, there are so many memories that bring a smile to my heart. Here are some of my fondest.

- The simple joy of picking wild violets or gathering hickory nuts with a grandparent.
- Being ill, missing school and getting strawberry ice cream.
- The first time I slept in a tent.
- Holidays with all the relatives joking, laughing, and eating.
- Catching "lightning bugs" and putting them in a bottle.
- Watching a favorite TV show with the family.

What are some of your favorite memories of laughter and love?

1. _____

_____

2. _____

_____

3. _____

_____

4. _____

_____

5. _____

_____

6. _____

_____

7. _____

_____

8. _____

_____

9. _____

_____

There is hope for any woman who can look in a mirror and laugh at what she sees.

To help pull yourself out of the pit, reach out to someone else.

The things you can do to celebrate are unlimited. Here are three inexpensive ideas you may want to adapt or use to create your own celebrations.

- Call up a friend and invite her over to bake cookies or make candy with you. Then giftwrap what you make and take it to someone who would really appreciate it.
- Forget the hassle. Celebrate Saturday as a day off from your regular workweek. Have a celebration breakfast. Fix specialties your family likes, or you may even want to invite friends over for waffles, pancakes, or special omeletes.
- Select a rainy day and invite a friend over for tea, or make it for lunch, if you like. Set the table with white linen, flowers, and your favorite tea things. If you have a fireplace, why not set up a table in front of the fire.

Jot down some of your own celebration ideas.

1. _____

_____

2. _____

_____

3. _____

_____

4. _____

_____

5. _____

_____

6. _____

_____

7. _____

_____

8. _____

_____

All we need is an ear to listen, an eye to behold, and a heart to feel.

We're not put on this earth to see through
each other, but to see each other through.

I used to have a handle on life, but then it fell off!

Spring is God's way of saying "One more time!"

All that is worth cherishing in this world begins in the heart, not the head.

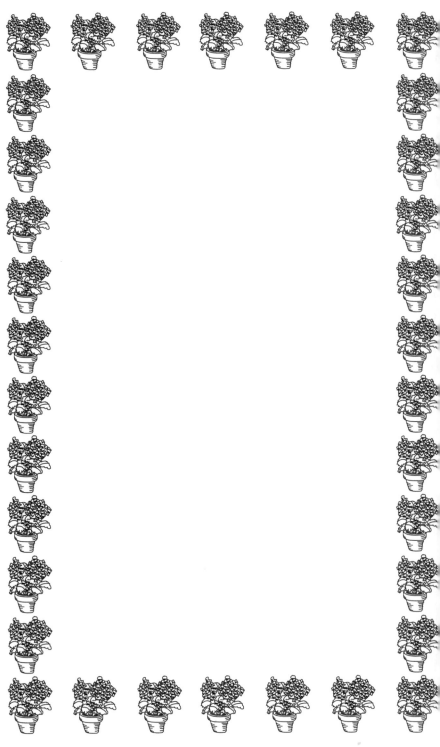

Remember, you are gold in the making.

_____

_____

_____

_____

_____

_____

_____

_____

The only condition for loving is to love without condition.

_____

_____

_____

_____

_____

_____

_____

Always—and I mean always—TAKE TIME TO LAUGH! It is the music of the soul!

_____

_____

_____

_____

_____

_____

_____

_____

_____

_____

_____

_____

_____

_____

_____

Opportunities to refresh and encourage others are everywhere. Surely you know someone who is . . .

- In an unfamiliar situation, like a new job, or possibly away at school.
- Tired and weary of it all.
- Lonely, and wondering if anybody cares any more.
- Uncertain of the future because of poor health, job setbacks, or any number of other reasons.

If someone's name or face flashes to mind, jot down some practical ways that you can reach out to the person with love and kindness.

1. _____

2. _____

3. _____

4. _____

5. _____

Nobody cares how much you know unless they know how much you care.

A friend is one who knows all about you and loves you anyway.

_____

_____

_____

_____

_____

_____

_____

_____

Love is warm arms instead of cold shoulders.

_____

_____

_____

_____

_____

Whenever we face difficult situations in life, we can ask God to help us. That is what the psalmist did. Here is a list of sample prayers from the Psalms to help in times of need.

distress—Psalm 4:1; 31:9

agony—Psalm 6:2

persecution by enemies—Psalm 19:13; 56:1

loneliness and affliction—Psalm 25:16

disaster—Psalm 57:1

weakness and trouble—Psalm 41:1; 86:16

sin itself—Psalm 51:1

Look for psalms that speak to other specific needs and write them down here:

1. _____

_____

2. _____

_____

3. _____

_____

4. _____

_____

5. _____

_____

6. _____

_____

7. _____

_____

8. _____

_____

9. _____

_____

10. _____

_____

Experience is what you get when you're looking for something else.

Laughter is to life what salt is to an egg.

We don't laugh because we're happy;
we're happy because we laugh.

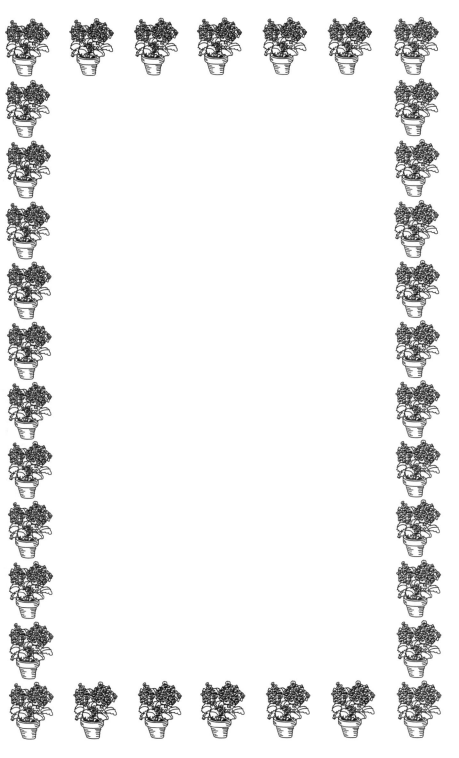

Love makes the world go 'round, but laughter keeps you from getting dizzy.

Tact is rubbing out another's mistake instead of rubbing it in.

Talking is sharing . . . listening is caring.

_____

_____

_____

_____

_____

_____

_____

_____

_____

_____

_____

_____

_____

_____

_____

_____

_____

_____

Laughter is good for our mental health. And laughing at embarrassing moments is a great way to find things to laugh about.

Write about one of the funniest "most-embarrassing moments" in your life and have fun laughing about it!

The black tarpaulin of depression hides God's sunshine of hope from our view.

_____

_____

_____

_____

_____

_____

_____

_____

God will never lead you where his strength cannot keep you.

_____

_____

_____

_____

_____

_____

If at first you don't succeed, see
if the loser gets anything.

Some days you're the bug . . . some days
the windshield!

What to Do in Case of Emergency

1. Pick up your hat.

2. Grab your coat.

3. Leave your worries on the doorstep.

4. Direct your feet to the sunny side of the street.

Hope is faith holding out its hand in the dark.

_____

_____

_____

_____

_____

_____

_____

_____

What we weave in time we must wear in eternity.

_____

_____

_____

_____

_____

_____

How long has it been since you did some fun, childlike things? Like . . .

- Eating watermelon on the front steps.
- Jumping into a pile of autumn leaves.
- Gathering big armfuls of lilacs to bring to a friend.
- Going up on the down escalator.

Make a list of some simple things you could do to break out of your little plastic mold . . . and have some fun!

1. _____

2. _____

3. _____

4. _____

5. _____

6. _____

I don't mind the rat race but I could do with a little more cheese.

_____

_____

_____

_____

_____

_____

_____

Advice is like snow, the softer it falls, the deeper it sinks.

_____

_____

_____

_____

_____

_____

_____

When your dreams turn
to dust—vacuum!

Practical guide for successful living: Put your head under the pillow and scream.

When it's all said and done . . .
there is only one thing we can do:
FROM THIS MOMENT ON . . .
LOVE.

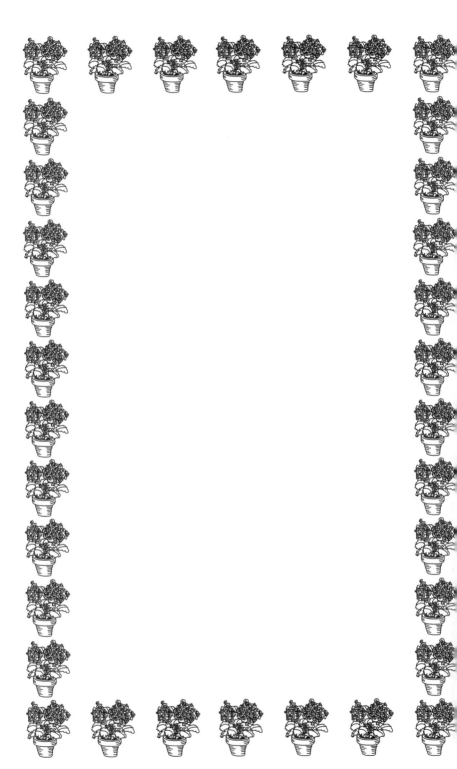

Send a postcard to the Geranium Lady!

Barbara Johnson spends her days spreading cheer and kindness to others. Now you can send some of that cheer right back to her. Write a note to warm her heart and brighten her day—then send her your splash of joy!

Barbara Johnson
P.O. Box 444
La Habra, CA
90633-0444

Place
postage
here

Dear Barbara,